FRANCHISING IN NIGERIA 2014

Legal and Business Considerations

KENDAL H. TYRE, JR., EXECUTIVE EDITOR
DIANA VILMENAY-HAMMOND, MANAGING EDITOR
COURTNEY L. LINDSAY, II, ASSISTANT EDITOR

LEXNOIR FOUNDATION

FIRST QUARTER 2014

LexNoir Foundation is the charitable, educational arm of LexNoir, an international network of lawyers connecting the African Diaspora.

This publication, *Franchising in Nigeria 2014: Legal and Business Considerations*, contains excerpts from *Franchising in Africa 2014: Legal and Business Considerations*. Both works are published by LexNoir Foundation and reflect the points of view of the authors and editors as of the date of publication and do not necessarily represent the opinions, interpretations, or positions of the law firms or organizations with which they are affiliated, nor the opinions, interpretations or positions of LexNoir Foundation or LexNoir.

Nothing contained in this book is to be considered as the rendering of legal advice, either generally or in connection with any specific issues or case. Readers are responsible for obtaining advice from their own legal counsel or other professional. This book, any forms and agreements or other information herein are intended for educational and informational purposes only.

Table of Contents

Franchising in Nigeria

Theophilus Emuwa and Tiwalola Okeyinka
ÆLEX

Bibliography of International Franchise Resources

Kendal H. Tyre, Jr., Diana Vilmenay-Hammond, Pierce Haesung Han, Courtney L. Lindsay, II, and Keri McWilliams
Nixon Peabody LLP

Acknowledgment

This book could not have been written without the hard work and dedication of each of the contributing authors and editors. Thank you.

We would like to acknowledge and extend our heartfelt gratitude to Michael Collier and Maria Stallings of the Washington, D.C. office of Nixon Peabody LLP for their invaluable assistance in revising, proofing, and editing this publication.

About the Editors and Authors

Kendal H. Tyre, Jr. – Kendal is a partner in the Washington, D.C. office of Nixon Peabody LLP. He handles domestic and cross-border transactions, including mergers and acquisitions, joint ventures, strategic alliances, licensing, and franchise matters.

In his franchise and licensing practice, Kendal counsels domestic and international franchisors, franchisees, licensors, licensees and distributors regarding U.S. state and federal franchise laws as well as foreign franchise legislation in a variety of jurisdictions. Kendal drafts and provides advice with regard to franchise and license agreements, disclosure documents and area development agreements and has extensive experience drafting and negotiating a variety of other commercial agreements. His client base spans the United States and foreign countries, including South Africa, Kenya, and the United Kingdom.

Kendal is a frequent contributor to franchise publications and a frequent speaker at franchise programs held by the American Bar Association Forum on Franchising and the International Franchise Association.

Kendal is co-chair of the firm's Diversity Action Committee and its Africa Group. Kendal is also the executive director of LexNoir Foundation.

E-mail address: ktyre@nixonpeabody.com

Diana Vilmenay-Hammond – Diana is an attorney in the Washington, D.C. office of Nixon Peabody LLP. She is a member of the firm's Franchise & Distribution Team.

In her franchise practice, Diana works with domestic and international franchisors on transactional and litigation matters. Specifically, she counsels franchisor clients regarding state and federal franchise laws, disclosure and registration obligations.

Diana drafts and negotiates various commercial agreements, including international franchise and development agreements.

Diana has co-authored numerous articles on franchising and frequently co-hosted the Nixon Peabody franchise law webinar series. Topics have included:

- "Franchise Case Law Round-Up: Implications for Your Franchise," February 15, 2012;
- "Social Media Part II: Best Practices in Protecting Your Brand in the New Media," September 14, 2010; and
- "The Awuah Case: Bellwether or Outlier," May 11, 2010

Diana received her J.D. from Howard University School of Law and her B.A. from Georgetown University. She is a member of the American Bar Association (Forum on Franchising).

Email address: dvilmenay@nixonpeabody.com

Pierce Haesung Han – Pierce is an associate in Nixon Peabody's Global Business & Transactions Group. Pierce focuses his practice on three main areas, assisting clients with a variety of complex business transactions.

- Mergers & Acquisitions: Providing assistance to both public and private clients with various mergers and acquisitions, performing due diligence, drafting and negotiating transaction documents, and facilitating closing and post-closing mechanics.
- International Commercial Transactions: Drafting and negotiating a variety of commercial agreements, including international franchise and development agreements, license agreements, and purchase and sale agreements.
- Federal Securities Law Matters: Assisting public and private clients regarding federal securities laws and stock exchange rules relating to corporate governance and disclosure.

Pierce serves as the Secretary of the Asian Pacific Bar Association Educational Fund (an affiliate of the Asian Pacific American Bar Association of the Greater Washington, D.C. Area).

Pierce received his J.D. from Georgetown University Law Center and his B.A. from Case Western Reserve University. He is admitted to practice in the State of New York and the District of Columbia.

E-mail address: phan@nixonpeabody.com

Courtney L. Lindsay, II – Courtney is an associate in Nixon Peabody's Corporate and Finance practice. In his corporate practice, Courtney assists for-profit and non-profit entities with transactional matters and corporate governance. In various capacities, Courtney has been involved in multiple merger and acquisition transactions, including drafting and managing due diligence.

Previously, Courtney worked in the legal and business affairs department at a national cable network, where he handled matters related to the network's LLC agreement, including drafting board and member consent agreements.

Courtney received his J.D. from the University of Virginia School of Law and his B.A. from the University of Virginia. He is admitted to practice in the Commonwealth of Virginia and the District of Columbia.

E-mail address: clindsay@nixonpeabody.com

Keri McWilliams – Keri is an associate in the Franchise & Distribution team of Nixon Peabody LLP. Keri works with clients on a number of franchising issues, including obtaining and maintaining franchise registrations in various states, responding to state inquiries regarding trade practices, ongoing compliance with state and federal regulations, and updating franchise disclosure documents. She also handles franchise sales counseling and franchise system issues.

Keri is a member of the American Bar Association's Forum on Franchising, and the Federal and Minnesota State bar associations. She is also a member of Minnesota Women Lawyers and the Minnesota Association of Black Lawyers, and a volunteer in the Volunteer Lawyers Network.

Keri received her J.D. from the Georgetown University Law Center and her B.F.A. from Washington University. She is admitted to practice in the District of Columbia and Minnesota.

E-mail address: kmcwilliams@nixonpeabody.com

Theophilus I. Emuwa – Theo is a partner at AELEX in Lagos, Nigeria focused on commercial law. He is widely acknowledged as one of Nigeria's leading tax practitioners. He regularly advises on Nigerian companies income and petroleum profits tax issues, corporate structures, shareholder rights and other corporate governance issues. Theo has provided advice on privatization options and strategies for clients, reviewed business process and procedures for operating in the petroleum sector, led several due diligence reviews and advised on environmental matters and compensation issues after an oil spill.

Theo is an active member of International Trademark Association (INTA) and is on the editorial board of the Trademark Reporter, a journal of the INTA. He is the author of the Nigeria section of the International Annual Review of Trademark Jurisprudence (also published by the INTA) and a member of the Intellectual Property Lawyers' Association of Nigeria. Theo is also a member of the section on intellectual property, communications and technology law of the IBA and the Intellectual Property Law Association of Nigeria. Theo is admitted to practice law in England and Wales, Nigeria and Ghana.

E-mail address: tiemuwa@aelex.com

Tiwalola Okeyinka – Tiwalola is an associate at AELEX in Lagos, Nigeria focused on energy and natural resources. She was part of the team that drafted and advised on Gas

Transportation Agreements, Gas Sales Agreements and Heads of Terms for clients within the Oil and Gas Industry. She has advised on franchise agreements, NOTAP registration in Nigeria and labour and employment issues in Nigeria. She is currently on the team advising on the construction of a hydroelectric power plant in Nigeria.

E-mail address: tokeyinka@aelex.com

About the Book

Franchising in Nigeria 2014: Legal and Business Considerations contains excerpts from the larger work, *Franchising in Africa 2014: Legal and Business Considerations.* Both books serve as practical, succinct, easy-to-use reference tools for lawyers, business people and academics to use in navigating the myriad laws and business issues impacting franchise arrangements on the African continent.

This book provides an overview of the franchise industry in Nigeria and addresses the typical legal issues confronted when expanding a franchise system in Nigeria. The larger work, *Franchising in Africa 2014: Legal and Business Considerations,* covers those laws governing franchising in fifteen other African countries – Angola, Botswana, Burundi, Cape Verde, Democratic Republic of Congo, Egypt, Ethiopia, Ghana, Kenya, Mozambique, Rwanda, South Africa, Tunisia, Zambia and Zimbabwe.

In both books, an author, who is a legal expert in the designated jurisdiction, addresses the basic questions that a franchise lawyer would need to know to competently represent a client in expanding their franchise system to that country.

Each country chapter organizes a discussion of that country's laws under various headings and in a uniform format. Topics were sent to each country's author in the form of a questionnaire, and each author drafted responses to the questions presented. A general overview relating to the political and economic history of the country at the beginning of each chapter provides an initial context for the regulatory framework. [1]

---

[1] The source of information for these sections is the Central Intelligence Agency, https://www.cia.gov/library/publications/the-world-factbook/ (last visited November 3, 2013).

Apart from an overview of the legal framework for franchising, each book contains other articles and resources that should prove useful to those in the franchise industry.

The authors for each chapter are listed at the beginning of a chapter and their biographical information is listed in the previous section, *About the Editors and Authors*.

Readers should always consult with local counsel in the relevant jurisdiction instead of relying solely on the information contained in this book. The laws governing franchising are evolving and local counsel in Nigeria are best positioned to provide timely, relevant advice applying the current law to the particular facts of a case.

Franchising in Nigeria

Theophilus Emuwa and Tiwalola Okeyinka

ÆLEX

Lagos, Nigeria

Nigeria

I.   Introduction

A.   Historical Background of Country

A series of constitutions after World War II granted Nigeria greater autonomy; independence came in 1960. Following nearly 16 years of military rule, a new constitution was adopted in 1999, and a peaceful transition to civilian government was completed. The government continues to face the daunting task of reforming a petroleum-based economy, whose revenues have been squandered through corruption and mismanagement, and institutionalizing democracy. In addition, Nigeria continues to experience longstanding ethnic and religious tensions. Although both the 2003 and 2007 presidential elections were marred by significant irregularities and violence, Nigeria is currently experiencing its longest period of civilian rule since independence. The general elections of April 2007 marked the first civilian-to-civilian transfer of power in the country's history.

B.   Economy of the Country

Nigeria has undertaken several reforms over the past decade. Nigeria's former military rulers failed to diversify the economy away from its overdependence on the capital-intensive oil sector, which provides 95% of foreign exchange earnings and about 80% of budgetary revenues. Since 2008, the government has begun showing the political will to implement the market-oriented reforms urged by the IMF, such as to modernize the banking system, to curb inflation by blocking excessive wage demands, and to resolve regional disputes over the distribution of earnings from the oil industry. In 2003, the government began deregulating fuel prices, announced the privatization of the country's four oil refineries, and instituted the National Economic Empowerment Development Strategy, a domestically designed and run program modeled on the IMF's Poverty Reduction and Growth Facility for fiscal and monetary management. In November 2005, Abuja won Paris Club[2]

Nigeria

approval for a debt-relief deal that eliminated US$18 billion of debt in exchange for US$12 billion in payments—a total package worth US$30 billion of Nigeria's total US$37 billion external debt. The deal subjects Nigeria to stringent IMF reviews. Based largely on increased oil exports and high global crude prices, GDP rose strongly in 2007–09.

GDP rose strongly in 2007-11 because of growth in non-oil sectors and robust global crude oil prices. President Goodluck Jonathan has established an economic team that includes experienced and reputable members and has announced plans to increase transparency, diversify economic growth, and improve fiscal management. Lack of infrastructure and slow implementation of reforms are key impediments to growth. The government is working toward developing stronger public-private partnerships for roads, agriculture, and power. Nigeria's financial sector was hurt by the global financial and economic crises, but the Central Bank governor has taken measures to restructure and strengthen the sector to include imposing mandatory higher minimum capital requirements.

C.   Franchise Legal Overview

Currently, Nigeria's general commercial laws govern the rights and obligations of parties to a franchise agreement. Nigeria does not have franchise specific legislation but it has enacted legislation governing the importation of intellectual property. Any agreement relating to the importation of intellectual property must be registered with Nigeria's National Office for Technology Acquisition and Promotion ("NOTAP"). NOTAP has a number of specifications that must be satisfied before it will register any agreement. According to trade publications, franchise opportunities in the country include, not only food franchising but also retail, telecommunications, oil and gas, banking and hospitality. To promote franchising activity in the

---

[2]   A monthly meeting in Paris attended by creditors of 19 countries to discuss debt issues. Among other things, the Paris Club addresses the issue of coordinated debt relief for developing countries that cannot service their debt.

country, the Nigerian International Franchise Association ("NIFA") assists franchisors and potential franchisees by providing services such as financial and marketing advice, consulting, franchise recruitment and feasibility studies.

II.   Regulatory Requirements

A.   Pre-Sale Disclosure

Please describe any pre-sale franchise disclosure or similar requirements that may apply to franchise transactions.

No pre-sale franchise disclosure or similar requirements apply to franchise transactions under the laws of Nigeria.

B.   Governmental Approvals, Registrations, Filing Requirements

Please describe any necessary government approvals, registrations, or filing requirements that may apply to franchise transactions.

NOTAP is charged with the responsibility of registering all agreements entered into for the transfer of foreign technology to Nigerian parties.

Section 4 of the *National Office for Technology Acquisition and Promotion Act*[3] ("NOTAP Act") states that such agreements are registrable if their purpose or intent is, in the opinion of the NOTAP, wholly or partially for or in connection with the following:

o   use of trademarks;

o   use of patented inventions;

o   supply of technical expertise in the form of technical assistance of any description whatsoever;

---

[3]   *Chapter N62 Laws of the Federation of Nigeria* ("LFN") 2004.

Nigeria

o   supply of detailed engineering drawings;

o   supply of machinery and plant; and

o   provision of operating staff, managerial assistance, and the training of personnel.

A franchisor entering into a franchise agreement with a Nigerian party will have to register the agreement with NOTAP. To qualify for registration, the franchise agreement must comply with the specifications provided under Section 6 (2) of the NOTAP Act. The franchise agreement must:

o   provide a transfer of technology not freely available in Nigeria;

o   provide pricing and other valuable consideration commensurate with the technology acquired or to be acquired;

o   not give the franchisor powers to regulate or intervene in the administration of any undertaking belonging to the franchisee;

o   not oblige the franchisee to onerously or gratuitously assign to the franchisor or any designated persons, patents, trademarks, technical information, innovations, or improvements obtained by such franchisee with no assistance from the franchisor or such person;

o   not impose limitations on technological research or development by the franchisee;

o   not require the franchisee to acquire equipment, tools, parts, or raw materials exclusively from the franchisor or any other person or given source;

o   not prohibit or restrict the exportation of the franchisee's products or services;

o   not compel or oblige the franchisee to sell the products manufactured by it exclusively to the franchisor or any designated person or source;

o   allow the franchisee to use complementary technologies;

o   not compel the franchisee to use personnel designated by the franchisor either on a permanent basis or for any unconscionable period;

o   not require the franchisee to appoint the franchisor as the exclusive sales agent;

o   not exceed a period of ten years;

o   not oblige the franchisee to introduce unnecessary design changes;

o   not permit the franchisor to impose unnecessary and onerous obligations on the franchisee by means of quality controls or prescription of standards;

o   not require the franchisee to pay in full for transferred technology that has not been exploited by the franchisee;

o   not compel the franchisee to accept additional technology or other matter, such as consultancy services, international sub-contracting, turn-key projects, and similar package arrangements not required by the franchisee for or in connection with the principal purpose for which technology is to be or has been acquired by franchisee; or

o   not oblige the franchisee to submit to foreign jurisdiction in any controversy arising from a decision concerning the interpretation or enforcement in Nigeria of any such contract or agreement or any provisions thereof.

NOTAP may register a franchise agreement notwithstanding the above specifications, if it is in the "national interest"[4] to do so.

Nigeria

Where the franchise would involve the use of the franchisor's trademark in the business in Nigeria, and it is intended that the franchise agreement be registered with NOTAP, the application for registration would have to be accompanied by evidence of the franchisor's right to those trademarks. A schedule of the trademarks and logo (where applicable) will suffice. *See also* Section III (Currency) of this chapter relating to bank approvals potentially required to authorize or effect transfers of payments due under a franchise agreement.

The documents required for filing a franchise agreement with NOTAP include:

o   Duly completed NOTAP application form

o   List and proof of patent/trademark registration;

o   Two (2) copies of NOTAP Questionnaire duly completed;

o   Two (2) certified copies (by company secretary of the franchisee) of the franchise agreement to be registered;

o   Certificate of incorporation of the franchisee;

o   Memorandum and articles of association of the franchisee;

o   Audited accounts for 3 years of the franchisee;

o   List of expatriates and Nigerian understudy; and

o   Comprehensive training schedule indicating number of personnel, place, duration and the skill or knowledge to be acquired.

NOTAP may sometimes perform an inspection of an applicant's premises prior to granting approval of an agreement which has

---

[4]   Section 6 (3) NOTAP Act.

been submitted to it. Where NOTAP decides to do an inspection, approval may not be obtained until about a month after the inspection. Where NOTAP decides not to do a prior inspection, it typically takes about a month from the submission of the agreement to receive a response from NOTAP, possibly with approval.

C. Limits of Fees and Typical Term of Franchise Agreement

Please describe any limits upon the nature and extent of fees and the term of a typical franchise agreement.

1. Limits on Nature of Fees

a. Royalty Fees

The *Revised Guidelines on Acquisition of Foreign Technology* published by NOTAP in 2003 ("NOTAP Guidelines") stipulates that royalty fees in connection with trademark and know-how agreements, including franchise agreements, should not exceed 5% of the net sale value or profit before tax, where net sales value is not applicable. Net sales value is defined as the ex-factory sales price of the product, exclusive of excise duties and other taxes less the cost of the standard bought-out components and the landed cost of imported components, irrespective of the source of procurement, including freight, insurance, and custom duties. In practice, net sales value is interpreted to mean turnover.

However, in practice, NOTAP may not approve an agreement where royalty fees exceed 2.5% of the turnover of the franchisee. Also, NOTAP will not approve payment of trademark fees to be made in respect of any agreement where the trademark owner has more than 75% of the equity in the local company.

The NOTAP Guidelines state that where the Nigerian enterprise is acquiring the right to practice a process, the concept of know-how should be clearly expressed and defined in the contract. In this connection, the franchisor cannot charge a separate fee for concepts such as "technical information" or "technical services." It also provides that agreements that include provisions for payments for the use of foreign trademark will not be accepted for registration except if the trademark is internationally recognized and the product is meant for export.

b.   Technical Services Fees

Fees for technical services must not be tied to sales or profit; instead they must be calculated on a per diem rate or man-hour, man-day, or man-month.

c.   Management Fees

Management fees must not exceed 5% of profit before tax except for the management of hotels by international hotel chains, in which case a basic or lump sum fee not exceeding 5% of turnover plus an incentive fee not exceeding 12% of gross operating profit ("GOP") is currently applicable.

d.   Consultancy Fees

Consultancy fees must not exceed 5% of the total project cost and must be limited to projects of very high technology content for which indigenous expertise is not available.

2.   The term of a typical franchise agreement

Parties are at liberty to negotiate the term of their franchise agreement. NOTAP Guidelines provide that the term of a franchise agreement to be registered with NOTAP must not exceed ten years. In practice, NOTAP may not approve agreements with a duration exceeding three years. The NOTAP registration can be renewed for a further period.

Nigeria

III. Currency

If all payments under a franchise agreement must be made in immediately available U.S. Dollars, please advise as to any restrictions, reporting requirements, or regulations concerning the exchange, repatriation, or remittance of U.S. Dollars.

The certificate of registration issued by NOTAP will be required by the Central Bank of Nigeria to authorize or effect transfer of any payment due to the franchisor under the franchise agreement. Remittance of fees shall be made by an authorized dealer and is subject to submission and acceptance of the following basic documentation:

o   a duly completed Form "A";

o   a certified copy of the franchise agreement registered by NOTAP;

o   a certificate of registration issued by NOTAP;

o   a demand note from the franchisor;

o   evidence of payment of tax on the amount to be remitted;

o   an audited account for the relevant period; and

o   a certificate of satisfactory completion of the job issued by the Nigerian employer (applicable only to management fee and consultancy fees).

An authorized dealer is any bank licensed under the *Banks and Other Financial Institutions Act 1991*.[5] A completed Form "A" provides the particulars of the payee/applicant and the beneficiary, the purpose of the payment, and amount to be paid. It also contains a declaration by the applicant that the foreign

---

[5]   Chapter B3 LFN 2004.

Nigeria

currency will be used for the purpose stated in the form. See Appendix for example of Form "A."

IV. Taxes, Tariffs, and Duties

Please do not provide any in-depth comments on tax structuring. However, please provide your general comments on the typical amount of withholding tax that would apply and whether a "gross-up" provision contained in a franchise agreement would be enforceable in your country.

A. Applicable Rate

The applicable withholding tax rate for royalty payments made under a franchise agreement will be 10%. This tax exposure can be minimized if the party receiving the payments is incorporated in a country with which Nigeria has a double taxation agreement. Currently, Nigeria has signed and adopted double taxation agreements with the United Kingdom, France, Belgium, Pakistan, Romania, Canada, Czech Republic, China, Slovak Republic, The Netherlands, South Africa, and Italy. Nigeria has also negotiated and signed double taxation agreements with 7 other countries but the agreements have not been ratified/ adopted. The countries are Sweden, South Korea, Spain, Russia, Mauritius, Denmark, and Algeria.

B. Gross-up Clauses

Paragraph 2 of the *Companies Income Tax (Rates, Etc., of Tax Deducted at Source (Withholding Tax)) Regulations* made pursuant to the *Companies Income Tax Act*,[6] states that "a deduction made from a payment shall not be regarded as an additional cost of the contract to be included in the contract price but as tax due on the payment." A gross-up clause would be in violation of this regulation only if it provides that the person making payment under a contract would be obliged to pay any withholding tax or other statutory deductions in addition to the

---

[6]   Chapter C21 LFN 2004

Nigeria

contract price. Such a clause would be unenforceable. However, a gross-up clause that is drafted to state that the recipient would receive the amount it would have received prior to any deduction would be acceptable.

V.   Trademarks

Please advise us as to whether there are any special requirements for granting a valid trademark license, including the use of a registered user agreement or a short trademark license agreement and any required filing of such an agreement with the trademark authorities.

Section 33 of the *Trade Mark Act*[7] requires that a trademark license agreement or registered user agreement must be registered with the Nigerian Trademark Registry. Registration as a registered user confers the same rights as those of the proprietor of the trademark(s) except the right to assign or transfer. Also, subject to the terms of the agreement between the proprietor and the registered user, a registered user of a trademark is entitled to require that the proprietor institute proceedings to prevent infringement of the trademark(s) in respect of which a registered user status has been granted or to institute an action in his name if the proprietor refuses to take any action.

The Registrar of Trademarks is vested with the power to refuse the registration of a license agreement where it appears to the Registrar that the grant of registration will tend to facilitate trafficking in the trademark.

It will typically take about 4-6 weeks from filing to obtain registration for a license agreement.

---

[7]   Chapter T13 LFN 2004.

Nigeria

VI. Restrictions on Transfer

Please advise as to whether there are any restrictions (1) on a franchisor to restrict transfers by a master franchisee, any interest in a master franchisee, or the assets of the master franchisee or (2) the ability of a master franchisee to control and/or restrict transfers of a subfranchisee's rights under a master franchise agreement, interest in the subfranchisee, or the assets of the subfranchisee.

No. There are no restrictions on a franchisor to restrict transfers by a master franchisee, any interest in a master franchisee, or the assets of the master franchisee, or the ability of the master franchisee to control and/or restrict transfers of a subfranchisee's rights under a master franchise agreement, interest in the subfranchisee, or assets of the subfranchisee. It is typical for agreements to make provisions to the effect that the franchise agreement will terminate in the event of a material change in the structure or business of the company.

VII. Termination

Please advise us as to any laws relating to termination in your country, such as agency laws, required indemnity provisions, notice or "good cause" requirements, or other laws affecting termination of a franchise agreement. Please describe.

There are no laws regulating termination of franchise agreements in Nigeria. Most agency relationships in Nigeria are based on an express or implied agreement between the parties.[8] Parties have a right to terminate an agreement or deem an agreement to have been terminated once any of the grounds for termination stated in the agreement occurs.

An agency relationship may be terminated by mutual agreement between the principal and the agent or on the death, bankruptcy,

---

[8]   *Niger Progress Ltd v North East Line Corporation* (1989) 3 N.W.L.R. (PT.107) 68.

and/or insanity of either party. An agency relationship will also be terminated if its continuation becomes impossible, e.g., on grounds of frustration or a supervening impossibility.

If an agreement specifies a period of notice, the notice of termination must be for that period, but if no period is specified, a reasonable notice must be given. A principal who gives less notice than is reasonable may nevertheless succeed in terminating the relationship, but it will be deemed to have committed a breach of contract in doing so.

VIII. Governing Law, Jurisdiction, and Dispute Resolution

A.   Choice of Law of Foreign Jurisdiction

Please confirm whether the choice of law of a foreign jurisdiction would likely to be upheld under the law of the country, except for certain matters such as trademarks, bankruptcy, and competition matters, which we assume would be governed by the law in your country.

Under Nigerian law, in the absence of fraud or misrepresentation, parties are bound by the terms of their contract.[9] Contracting parties also have the freedom to choose the law that would regulate their transaction and the courts would generally uphold foreign choice of law clauses as long as these do not violate the provision of any Nigerian law.

However, where the agreement is to be registered with NOTAP, by virtue of Section 6 (2) of the NOTAP Act, NOTAP may refuse to register any agreement which compels the franchisee to submit to foreign jurisdiction in any controversy arising for decision concerning the interpretation or enforcement in Nigeria of any such contract or agreement or any provisions thereof.

---

[9]   *See Omoniyi v. Alabi* [2004] 6 NWLR (Pt. 870) 551.

Nigeria

B.   International Arbitration Dispute Resolution

Please confirm that a court in your country would honor an election of international arbitration dispute resolution, and therefore refuse to hear any disputes arising under a franchise agreement.

Once an agreement has been approved by NOTAP, a Nigerian court will honor an election of international arbitration dispute resolution.

Nigeria gives effect to some provisions of the *Convention on the Recognition and Enforcement of Foreign Arbitral Awards* (the "New York Convention") – to which it is a signatory.

IX.   Non-Competition Provisions

If the franchise agreement prohibits the master franchisee from engaging in certain competitive activities during the term of the agreement, and for a 12-month period after the termination or expiration of the agreement, please comment on the enforceability of non-competition covenants in your country.

Non-competition provisions that are unreasonable as regards the person restrained in terms of the duration and geographical area covered are generally unenforceable in Nigeria. With respect to franchise agreements, and as specified in Section II.B., NOTAP will not register any agreement which would:

o   require the franchisee to acquire equipment, tools, parts, or raw materials exclusively from the franchisor or any other person or given source;

o   prohibit or restrict the exportation of the franchisee's products or services;

o   compel or oblige the franchisee to sell the products manufactured by it exclusively to the franchisor or any designated person or source;

o   prevent the franchisee from using complementary technologies;

o   compel the franchisee to use personnel designated by the franchisor either on a permanent basis or for any unconscionable period; or

o   require the franchisee to appoint the franchisor as its exclusive sales agent.

X.   Language Requirements

Does the law in your country require that a franchise agreement be translated into the local language in order to be enforceable between the parties?

No. There is no law requiring a franchise agreement to be translated into a local language to be enforceable between the parties. However, agreements required or intended to be registered with NOTAP or any other regulatory body must be in the English language or must be accompanied by its English interpretation notarized in the country of origin.

XI.   Other Significant Matters

Please advise as to whether there are any significant matters not addressed above of which a franchisor should be aware in connection with its entering into a franchise agreement in your country.

Policy arguments notwithstanding, many franchisors may object to any or all of the NOTAP specifications and may want to consider alternatives. One such alternative is to structure contracts around objectionable provisions of the NOTAP Act. For example, although NOTAP might take the position that the

Nigeria

know-how and intellectual property rights being licensed by a franchisor are not valuable enough to Nigeria to justify a license fee at the upper end of the 5% range, in order to avoid such agreements being refused, applicants have in the past broken up fees into smaller and separate fees, e.g., a royalty fee for know-how, another fee for technical assistance, and a fee for a trademark license. However, in recent times such applications have not succeeded.

A more complete solution may be available to franchisors negotiating with Nigerian franchisees that have assets and/or accounts outside of Nigeria. In such cases, contractual provisions may be drafted that require the franchisee to remit royalties to the franchisor via offshore accounts, thereby obviating the need to go through the local Nigerian banking systems and, in turn, making it unnecessary to register agreements with NOTAP altogether.

Local Franchise Association

Please reference the existence of any franchise association in your country and its principal contact.

The local franchise association in Nigeria is the Nigerian International Franchise Association ("NIFA"). There is no legal requirement that a franchisor become a member. The website address of NIFA is www.nigerianfranchise.org and e-mails can also be sent to nifa@nigerianfranchise.org or info@nigerianfranchise.org.

Franchise Specific Legislation in Nigeria

Please provide any insight as to any proposed franchise specific legislation that may be under consideration in your jurisdiction.

There are no proposed franchise specific legislations under consideration in Nigeria.

Franchise Brands in Nigeria

16

Nigeria

Please provide a sample of the franchised brands that operate in your country.

Some of the franchise brands in Nigeria include:

a.   Fast food/restaurant

- Dominos
- Steers
- Cold Stone Creamery
- Johnny Rockets
- Ocean Basket
- Debonairs
- Kentucky Fried Chicken
- Butterfields
- Barcelos
- Mugg & Bean
- Creamy Inn Ice Cream
- Chicken Inn
- Southern Fried Chicken

b.   Clothing and accessories

- Woolworths
- Mango
- Truworths
- Etam
- Zara outlet
- Mr. Price
- T.M. Lewin
- Nike
- Adidas
- Levi's
- United Colours by Benetton
- Wrangler

c.   Beauty

- Black Up cosmetics
- MUD Cosmetics

Nigeria

d.   Hotels

- Protea Hotels
- Hilton Hotels
- Meridien Hotels
- Southern Sun
- Best Western Hotel
- Intercontinental Hotels
- Radisson Blu
- Sheraton Hotels
- Hawthorn Suites by Wyndham
- Sun International

e.   Supermarkets

- Shoprite
- Game

f.   Car Rental services

- Hertz
- Avis

Appendix:
Nigeria – Form A

FEDERAL REPUBLIC OF NIGERIA
FOREIGN EXCHANGE (MONITORING/MISCELLANEOUS PROVISIONS)
DECREE 1995

FORM A

VALID FOR FOREX? (Y/N)	YEAR	ORIGINAL APPLICATION NUMBER AA 00056

(FOR INVISIBLE TRADE TRANSACTIONS)
(TO BE COMPLETED IN DUPLICATE)

Authorized Dealer's Code

*Please fill in appropriate information in the blank spaces provided
*Use capital letters throughout this form

1. _____
   Name and address of Applicant's Banker (Authorized Dealer)

2. PARTICULARS OF APPLICANT
APPLICANT'S NAME: _____
   (Surname First, where applicable)
ADDRESS: _____
   (P.O. Box is not acceptable)
TOWN: _____ STATE: _____ PHONE/FAX: _____
PASSPORT/REGISTRATION/CERTIFICATE OF INCORPORATION NUMBER_____
*AIR TICKET NUMBER: _____ AIRLINE: _____
*ROUTE: _____
*Complete only where applicable

3. PARTICULARS OF BENEFICIARY
BENEFICIARY'S NAME: _____
ADDRESS: _____
   (P.O. Box is not acceptable)
TOWN: _____ STATE: _____ PHONE/FAX: _____
COUNTRY: _____ CODE: _____
PASSPORT/REGISTRATION/CERTIFICATE OF INCORPORATION NUMBER_____

4. PURPOSE OF PAYMENT

Sectorial Purpose Code: _____

5.
   AMOUNT APPLIED FOR IN FOREIGN CURRENCY   (IN WORDS)
AMOUNT: _____ Currency Code: _____
Exchange Rate: _____
Payment Mode: _____ Code: _____

7. APPLICANT'S DECLARATION   AUTHORISED DEALER'S ENDORSEMENT
I/We declare that the above statements are true and that
the foreign currency will be used solely for the purpose
stated in accordance with the approved guidelines.   Stamp, Signature & Date
** Any false declaration will make me/us liable for
   prosecution   Full Name:_____

Stamp, Signature & Date

Full Name:_____

OFFICIAL USE ONLY
Amount Approved: _____ Currency Code: _____

Approving Officer's Signature & Date
Full Name: _____
Status: _____

Bibliography of International Franchise Resources

Kendal H. Tyre, Jr., Diana Vilmenay-Hammond, Pierce Haesung Han, Courtney L. Lindsay, II, and Keri McWilliams

Nixon Peabody LLP

Washington, D.C.

I.   General International Resources

Mark Abell, Gary R. Duvall, and Andrea Oricchio Kirsh, *International Franchise Legislation* B1, ABA FORUM ON FRANCHISING (1996)

Kathleen C. Anderson and Anthony M. Stiegler, *Put Muscle in Your Marks: Enforcing Intellectual Property Rights* W14, ABA FORUM ON FRANCHISING (1995)

Richard M. Asbill and Jane W. LaFranchi, *International Franchise Sales Laws—A Survey* W7, ABA FORUM ON FRANCHISING (2005)

Jeffery A. Brimer, Alison C. McElroy, and John Pratt, *Going International: What Additional Restraints Will You Face?* W4, ABA FORUM ON FRANCHISING (2011)

Michael G. Brennan, Alexander Konigsberg, and Philip F. Zeidman, *Globetrotting: A Workshop on International Franchising* 10/W8, ABA FORUM ON FRANCHISING (1994)

Michael G. Brennan, Alexander Konigsberg, and Philip F. Zeidman, *Globetrotting: Strategies for Launching U.S. Franchisors Abroad* 2/P2, ABA FORUM ON FRANCHISING (1994)

Christopher P. Bussert and Jennifer Dolman, *Regaining Your Trademark After Abandonment or Misappropriation* W7, ABA FORUM ON FRANCHISING (2011)

Ronald T. Coleman and Linda K. Stevens, *Trade Secrets and Confidential Information: Rights and Remedies* W2, ABA FORUM ON FRANCHISING (2000)

Finola Cunningham, *Commerce Department Helps Franchisors Go Global*, in FRANCHISING WORLD 63 (Dec. 2005)

Michael R. Daigle and Alex S. Konigsberg, *Meeting Off-Shore Disclosure and Contract Requirements* F/W13, ABA FORUM ON FRANCHISING (1992)

Jennifer Dolman, Robert A. Lauer, and Lawrence M. Weinberg, *Structuring International Master Franchise Relationships for Success and Responding When Things Go Awry* W22, ABA FORUM ON FRANCHISING (2007)

Gary R. Duvall, Paul Jones, and Jane LaFranchi, *Planning for the International Enforcement of Franchise Agreements* W6, ABA FORUM ON FRANCHISING (1999)

William Edwards, *International Expansion: Do Opportunities Outweigh Challenges?* in FRANCHISING WORLD (February 2008)

George J. Eydt and Stuart Hershman, *Bringing a Foreign Franchise System to the United States* W9, ABA FORUM ON FRANCHISING (2009)

William A. Finkelstein and Louis T. Pirkey, *International Trademarks* W15, ABA FORUM ON FRANCHISING (1991)

William A. Finkelstein, *Protecting Trademarks Internationally: Current Strategies and Developments* B3, ABA FORUM ON FRANCHISING (1996)

Stephen Giles, Lou H. Jones, and Lawrence Weinberg, *Negotiating and Documenting Complex International Franchise Agreements* W21, ABA FORUM ON FRANCHISING (2006)

Steven M. Goldman, Stephen Giles, Marc Israel, and Stanley Wong, *Competition Round Up from Around the World* LB2, ABA FORUM ON FRANCHISING (2004)

David C. Gryce and E. Lynn Perry, *Trademarks and Copyrights in the International Arena* 6/W4, ABA FORUM ON FRANCHISING (1993)

Kenneth S. Kaplan, Andrew P. Loewinger, and Penelope J. Ward, *System Standards in International Franchising* W14, ABA FORUM ON FRANCHISING (2005)

Edward Levitt and Jorge Mondragon, *A Survey of International Legal Traps and How to Avoid Them—Beyond the Franchise Laws* W20, ABA FORUM ON FRANCHISING (2007)

Ned Levitt, Kendal H. Tyre, and Penny Ward, *The Impossible Dream: Controlling Your International Franchise System* W4, ABA FORUM ON FRANCHISING (2010)

Michael K. Lindsey and Andrew P. Loewinger, *International (Non-U.S.) Franchise Disclosure Requirements* W9, ABA FORUM ON FRANCHISING (2002)

Andrew P. Loewinger and John Pratt, *Recent Changes and Trends in International Franchise Laws* W4, ABA FORUM ON FRANCHISING (2008)

Andrew P. Loewinger and Thomas M. Pitegoff, *Avoiding the Long Arm of the Law in International Franchising: Issues and Approaches* W8, ABA FORUM ON FRANCHISING (1995)

Craig J. Madson and Katherine C. Spelman, *Similarity and Confusion in the Intellectual Property Arena* W11, ABA FORUM ON FRANCHISING (1997)

Christopher A. Nowak, John Pratt, and Carl E. Zwisler, *Franchising Internationally with Countries with Opaque Legal Systems* W20, ABA FORUM ON FRANCHISING (2006)

E. Lynn Perry and John L. Sullivan Jr., *Trademark Compliance and Enforcement Techniques* E/W12, ABA FORUM ON FRANCHISING (1992)

Marcel Portmann, *Franchising Sector Proves Global Reach*, in FRANCHISING WORLD (January 2007)

John Pratt and Luiz Henrique O. do Amaral, *Civil Law for Common Law Practitioners (or How to Draft an Agreement for Use Overseas)* W4, ABA FORUM ON FRANCHISING (2002)

Kirk W. Reilly, Robert F. Salkowski and Geoffrey B. Shaw, *Determining the Rules of Engagement in Litigation Here and Abroad* W5, ABA FORUM ON FRANCHISING (2008)

Catherine Riesterer and Frank Zaid, *Basics of International Franchising* L/B2, ABA FORUM ON FRANCHISING (1997)

W. Andrew Scott and Christopher N. Wormald, *Stranger in a Strange Land: Contrasting Franchising in International Expansion* W2, ABA FORUM ON FRANCHISING (2003)

Donald Smith and Erik Wulff, *International Franchising: The Unraveling of an International Franchise Relationship* 15/W13, ABA FORUM ON FRANCHISING (1993)

Frank Zaid, Pamela Mills, and Michael Santa Maria, *Essential Issues in International Franchising* LB/1, ABA FORUM ON FRANCHISING (2001)

II. African Resources

Joyce G. Mazero and J. Perry Maisonneuve, *Franchising in the Middle East and North Africa* W2, ABA FORUM ON FRANCHISING (2009)

Kendal H. Tyre, Jr. and Diana Vilmenay-Hammond, *Franchise World: A Burgeoning Middle Class Spurs Franchise Investment in Africa*, MINORITY BUSINESS ENTREPRENEUR (November 2012)

Kendal H. Tyre, Jr., *IP Protection May Promote Additional Franchise Growth in Africa*, NIXON PEABODY LLP: FRANCHISING BUSINESS & LAW ALERT (September 2012)

Kendal H. Tyre, Jr., *Market Potential for Franchising in Africa*, NIXON PEABODY LLP: FRANCHISING BUSINESS & LAW ALERT (June 2011)

Kendal H. Tyre, Jr. and Courtney L. Lindsay, II, *Continued Growth of Franchising in Africa*, NIXON PEABODY LLP: FRANCHISE LAW ALERT (April 2013)

Kendal H. Tyre, Jr. and Courtney L. Lindsay, II, *Pan African Franchise Federation Holds Inaugural Meeting*, NIXON PEABODY LLP: AFRICA ALERT (June 2013)

Kendal H. Tyre, Jr. and Courtney L. Lindsay, II, *White House Encouraging Private Investment and Transparency in Sub-Saharan Africa*, NIXON PEABODY LLP: AFRICA ALERT (August 2012)

Kendal H. Tyre, Jr. and Diana Vilmenay-Hammond, *African Economic Growth Impacts Franchising on the Continent*, NIXON PEABODY LLP: FRANCHISE LAW ALERT (July 2012)

Kendal H. Tyre, Jr. and Diana Vilmenay-Hammond, *Franchising in Africa*, in FRANCHISING WORLD (August 2013)

John Sotos and Sam Hall, *African Franchising: Cross-Continent Momentum*, in FRANCHISING WORLD (June 2007)

A.   Angola

João Afonso Fialho, *Franchising in Angola*, in FRANCHISING IN AFRICA: LEGAL AND BUSINESS CONSIDERATIONS 91-105 (Kendal H. Tyre, Jr. & Diana Vilmenay-Hammond eds. 2012)

B.   Botswana

Bonzo Makgalemele, *Franchising in Botswana*, in FRANCHISING IN AFRICA: LEGAL AND BUSINESS CONSIDERATIONS 107-117 (Kendal H. Tyre, Jr. & Diana Vilmenay-Hammond eds. 2012)

C.   Cape Verde

João Afonso Fialho, *Franchising in Cape Verde*, in FRANCHISING IN AFRICA: LEGAL AND BUSINESS CONSIDERATIONS 119-132 (Kendal H. Tyre, Jr. & Diana Vilmenay-Hammond eds. 2012)

D.   Egypt

Girgis Abd El-Shahid, *Franchising in Eqypt*, in FRANCHISING IN AFRICA: LEGAL AND BUSINESS CONSIDERATIONS 133-142 (Kendal H. Tyre, Jr. & Diana Vilmenay-Hammond eds. 2012)

A. Safaa El Din El Oteifi, *Egypt*, in INTERNATIONAL FRANCHISING EGY/1 (Dennis Campbell gen. ed. 2011)

E.   Ethiopia

Yohannes Assefa and Biset Beyene Molla, *Franchising in Ethiopia*, in FRANCHISING IN AFRICA: LEGAL AND BUSINESS CONSIDERATIONS 143-157 (Kendal H. Tyre, Jr. & Diana Vilmenay-Hammond eds. 2012)

Kendal H. Tyre, Jr., Yohannes Assefa and Getachew Mengistie Alemu, *New Intellectual Property Regulation Requires Scramble to Protect Marks in Ethiopia*, NIXON PEABODY LLP: AFRICA ALERT (October 2013)

F.   Ghana

Divine K.D. Letsa and Hawa Tejansie Ajei, *Franchising in Ghana*, in FRANCHISING IN AFRICA: LEGAL AND BUSINESS CONSIDERATIONS 159-167 (Kendal H. Tyre, Jr. & Diana Vilmenay-Hammond eds. 2012)

G.   Libya

Kendal H. Tyre, Jr. & Diana Vilmenay-Hammond, *First U.S. Franchise Opens in Libya*, NIXON PEABODY LLP: AFRICA ALERT (August 2012)

H.   Mozambique

Diogo Xavier da Cunha, *Franchising in Mozambique*, in FRANCHISING IN AFRICA: LEGAL AND BUSINESS CONSIDERATIONS 169-182 (Kendal H. Tyre, Jr. & Diana Vilmenay-Hammond eds. 2012)

I.   Nigeria

Theo Emuwa and Bimbola Fowler-Ekar, *Franchising in Nigeria*, in FRANCHISING IN AFRICA: LEGAL AND BUSINESS CONSIDERATIONS 183-198 (Kendal H. Tyre, Jr. & Diana Vilmenay-Hammond eds. 2012)

Kendal H. Tyre, Jr. and Theo Emuwa, *Nigerian Franchising: Making Your Way Through the Thicket*, NIXON PEABODY LLP: FRANCHISE LAW ALERT (June 2005)

J.   South Africa

Eugene Honey, *Franchising and the New Consumer Protection Bill*, BOWMAN GILFILLAN (March 2008)

Eugene Honey, *Franchising and the Consumer Protection Bill*, BOWMAN GILFILLAN (May 2008)

Eugene Honey, *Pitfalls and Difficulties with the CPA*, ADAMS & ADAMS (March 2013)

Eugene Honey, *Disclosure is Compulsory*, ADAMS & ADAMS (May 2013)

Eugene Honey and Wim Alberts, *Fundamental Consumer Rights: The Right to Equality*, BOWMAN GILFILLAN (March 2009)

Eugene Honey and Wim Alberts, *The Reach of the Consumer Protection Bill: The Final*, BOWMAN GILFILLAN (March 2009)

Eugene Honey, *South Africa*, in GETTING THE DEAL THROUGH: FRANCHISE (2013) 172-178 (Philip F. Zeidman ed. 2013)

Taswell Papier, *Franchising in South Africa*, in FRANCHISING IN AFRICA: LEGAL AND BUSINESS CONSIDERATIONS 199-224 (Kendal H. Tyre, Jr. & Diana Vilmenay-Hammond eds. 2012)

Kendal H. Tyre, Jr., *A New Legal Landscape for Franchising in South Africa*, NIXON PEABODY LLP: FRANCHISING BUSINESS & LAW ALERT (September 2009)

K.   Tunisia

Yessine Ferah, *Franchising in Tunisia*, in FRANCHISING IN AFRICA: LEGAL AND BUSINESS CONSIDERATIONS 225-245 (Kendal H. Tyre, Jr. & Diana Vilmenay-Hammond eds. 2012)

Kendal H. Tyre, Jr., Diana Vilmenay-Hammond, and Yessine Ferah, *New Franchise Legislation in Tunisia*, NIXON PEABODY LLP: FRANCHISE LAW ALERT (September 2010)

L.   Zambia

Mabvuto Sakala, *Franchising in Zambia*, in FRANCHISING IN AFRICA: LEGAL AND BUSINESS CONSIDERATIONS 247-255 (Kendal H. Tyre, Jr. & Diana Vilmenay-Hammond eds. 2012)

www.ingramcontent.com/pod-product-compliance
Lightning Source LLC
Chambersburg PA
CBHW060325220326
41598CB00027B/4420